Take-Home Leveled Readers

On-level

Science

PEARSON
Scott Foresman

Editorial Offices: Glenview, Illinois • Parsippany, New Jersey • New York, New York
Sales Ofices: Needham, Massachusetts • Duluth, Georgia • Glenview, Illinois
Coppell, Texas • Sacramento, California • Mesa, Arizona

sfsuccessnet.com

ISBN: 0-328-19719-X

2 3 4 5 6 7 8 9 10 V004 13 12 11 10 09 08 07 06 05

Table of Contents

To the Teacher

Scott Foresman provides three Leveled Readers for every chapter of *Scott Foresman Science*, Grades 1–6: a *Below-Level Leveled Reader*, an *On-Level Leveled Reader*, and an *Advanced Leveled Reader*.

All three readers teach the same science concepts, same vocabulary, address the same target reading skill and contain the same graphic organizer as the corresponding student edition chapter, just at three different reading levels—providing access to important science content for all students. The On-level and Advanced readers also use additional examples to enrich the chapter and extend ideas

This book contains reproducible copies of the On-Level Leveled Readers for Grade 1. These are designed for you to reproduce and send home with your students as appropriate. Encourage students to share these books with parents or family members in order to practice reading skills and reinforce science content.

Online versions of these and other readers are also available through the Scott Foresman Leveled Reader Database.

Science

Genre	Comprehension Skill	Text Feature	Science Content
Nonfiction	Alike and Different	• Glossary	Living and Nonliving Things

Scott Foresman Science 1.1

ISBN 0-328-13734-0
9 780328 137343 90000

scottforesman.com

Life Science

Is It a Living Thing?

by Mary Katherine Tate

What did you learn?

1. What can all living things do?

2. What is a *need?*

3. **Writing** in Science Nonliving things are different than living things. Write to explain some of the ways they are different. Use words from the book as you write.

4. **Alike and Different** Plants and animals have needs. How are their needs alike? How are their needs different?

Vocabulary

living
nonliving
shelter

Picture Credits
Every effort has been made to secure permission and provide appropriate credit for photographic material. The publisher deeply regrets any omission and pledges to correct errors called to its attention in subsequent editions.

Photo locators denoted as follows: Top (T), Center (C), Bottom (B), Left (L), Right (R), Background (Bkgd).

2 Getty Images; 4 (B) ©Jerry Young/DK Images; 7 (C) ©Alan Watson/DK Images; 8 (TR) Digital Stock; 8 (L) Getty Images; 9 Georgette Douwma/ImageState.

ISBN: 0-328-13734-0

2 3 4 5 6 7 8 9 10 V004 13 12 11 10 09 08 07 06 05

Glossary

living something that is alive

nonliving something that was never alive

shelter a safe place

Is It a Living Thing?

by Mary Katherine Tate

Living Things

What are living things?
Living things are alive.

You can tell if something is a living thing. Is it alive? Can it change? Can it grow?

Living And Nonliving Things

Some things may look like living things.
They may move.
But they do not change and grow.
They are not living things.

Plants are alive.
Animals are alive.
People are alive.
These are all living things.

What Living Things Can Do

Living things can grow.
Living things can change.

People make some nonliving things.
These toys are nonliving.
Other nonliving things are in nature.
The water in the ocean is nonliving.

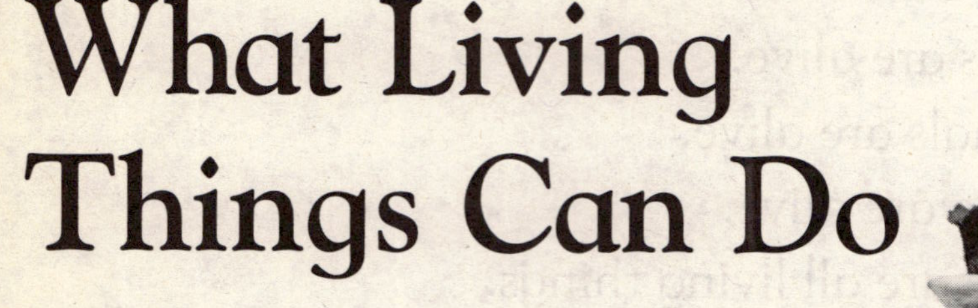

Nonliving things do not grow.
Nonliving things do not change on their own.

Some living things can move.
Some living things can have young living things.

Needs Of Living Things

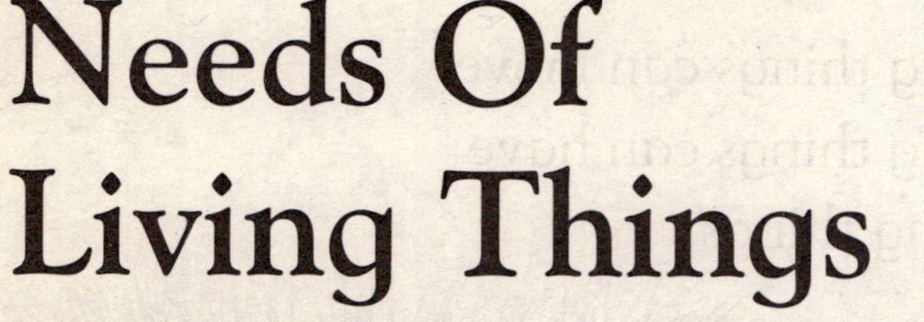

Living things have needs.
Needs are what living things must have to live.

These pails were never alive.
This hat was never alive.
Sand was never alive.
These are all nonliving things.

Nonliving Things

What are nonliving things?
Nonliving things were never alive.

What do plants need?

Plants need air.
They need water too.
Plants need light from the Sun.
They need space to grow.

What do animals need?

Animals need air.
They need water too.
Animals need food.

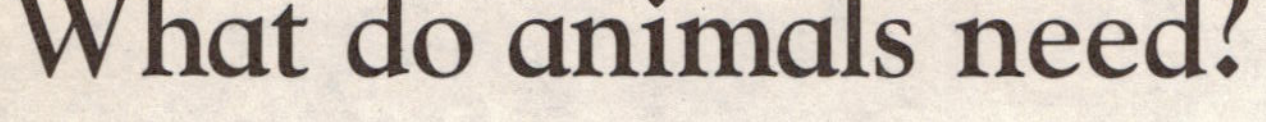

Animals need space to live.
A **shelter** is a safe place.
Animals need shelter.

Genre	Comprehension Skill	Text Features	Science Content
Nonfiction	Picture Clues	• Labels • Glossary	Habitats

Scott Foresman Science 1.2

scottforesman.com

Science

Science

Life Science

Places

by Mary Katherine Tate

Vocabulary

desert
forest
habitat
ocean
wetland

Picture Credits

Every effort has been made to secure permission and provide appropriate credit for photographic material. The publisher deeply regrets any omission and pledges to correct errors called to its attention in subsequent editions.

Photo locators denoted as follows: Top (T), Center (C), Bottom (B), Left (L), Right (R), Background (Bkgd).

Opener: (T) Digital Vision; 2 (TR, BL) Getty Images, (CL, CR) Digital Vision; 3 (CR) Mike Hill/Alamy Images; 5 Getty Images; 8 (Bkgd) Digital Vision; 10 (CR) Mike Hill/Alamy Images; 11 Getty Images; 12 (T, C) Getty Images; 13 Tom Bean/Corbis; 15 (TL, C) Digital Vision, (TR) Getty Images.

ISBN: 0-328-13737-5

2 3 4 5 6 7 8 9 10 V004 13 12 11 10 09 08 07 06 05

What did you learn?

1. What is a habitat?
2. What are three ways to describe oceans?
3. **Writing** in Science Plants and animals have ways to live in their habitats. Write to explain some ways grassland plants and animals live there. Use words from the book as you write.
4. **Picture Clues** Look at the pictures on pages 4–5. What do they tell you about the forest at different times of the year?

Glossary

desert a dry habitat

forest a habitat with many plants and trees

habitat a place where plants and animals live

ocean a saltwater habitat

wetland a habitat that is covered with water

Places

by Mary Katherine Tate

Habitats

All plants and animals need a place to live. A **habitat** is a place where plants and animals live.

Forest

Ocean

Grassland

Different Places

There are many different habitats. Different plants and animals live in different habitats. Habitats have what some plants and animals need.

Some grasses in grasslands can take lots of water from the ground. They can get the water they need when it is dry.

Wetland

Desert

A habitat has air. A habitat has food. A habitat has water. A habitat has shelter for some animals and plants.

There are different kinds of habitats. Some habitats are on land. Some habitats are in water.

Forests

Forest in summer

A **forest** is a land habitat. A forest has lots of trees. Forests have what some plants and animals need.

Bison

Living in a Grassland

Grasslands are big and open. They do not have much shelter for big animals. Some animals do not need it.

Some prairie animals stay in large groups. This helps them stay safe.

Grassland in summer

Grassland in winter

Grasslands Change

Grasslands can be different at different times of the year.

Prairies can be hot in the summer. They can be cold in the winter.

Forest in winter

Forests Change

A habitat can change. Habitats can be different at different times of the year.

Forest plants get a lot of sunlight in the summer. They get less light in the winter.

Wetlands

Wetland in summer

A **wetland** habitat is covered with water. Wetlands have what some plants and animals need.

Grasslands

A grassland is a land habitat. There are grasslands all over the world. Grasslands have what some plants and animals need.

One kind of grassland is a prairie. A prairie has tall grasses and other plants.

Kangaroo rat

Living in Habitats

Plants and animals in habitats have ways to live. Animals in deserts do not need much water. Living things in deserts have ways to live in sandy, dry places. Some desert rats can live a long time with no water. They can get water from seeds. Some plants can grow in sand.

Wetland in winter

Wetlands Change

Wetlands are different at different times of the year too. Wetlands get a lot of rain in the summer. They get less rain in the winter.

Oceans

An **ocean** is a water habitat. It has salt water. It is big and deep. Oceans have what some plants and animals need.

Deserts

A **desert** is a land habitat. It is very dry. It gets very little rain. Deserts have what some plants and animals need.

Science

Science

Genre	Comprehension Skill	Text Features	Science Content
Nonfiction	Alike and Different	• Call Outs • Captions • Labels • Glossary	Animals and Plants

Scott Foresman Science 1.3

PEARSON
Scott Foresman
scottforesman.com

ISBN 0-328-13740-5
9 780328 137404 90000

Life Science

Animals and Plants

by Shirley Horton

Vocabulary

antennae
camouflage
flower
leaf
root
stem

Picture Credits
Every effort has been made to secure permission and provide appropriate credit for photographic material. The publisher deeply regrets any omission and pledges to correct errors called to its attention in subsequent editions.

Photo locators denoted as follows: Top (T), Center (C), Bottom (B), Left (L), Right (R), Background (Bkgd)

2 Mitsuaki Iwago/Minden Pictures; 3 Fred Bavendam/Minden Pictures; 6 ©Jerry Young/DK Images; 8 Kevin Schafer/Corbis; 9 (C) Tom Vezo/Nature Picture Library, (BR) Jim Brandenburg/Minden Pictures; 13 (B) Mick Rock/Alamy Images; 15 ©Andrew Brown; Ecoscene/Corbis

ISBN: 0-328-13740-5

2 3 4 5 6 7 8 9 10 V004 13 12 11 10 09 08 07 06 05

What did you learn?

1. How does the fur of a polar bear help it live where it is cold?

2. How do goby fish help snapping shrimp?

3. **Writing** in Science Animals use camouflage to hide from danger. Write to explain how camouflage helps. Use words from the book as you write.

4. **Alike and Different** How are the danger calls of prairie dogs and rabbits alike? How are they different?

Glossary

antennae	feelers an animal uses to feel, smell, and taste
camouflage	a color or shape that makes a plant or an animal hard to see
flower	the part of the plant that makes seeds
leaf	the part of the plant that makes food
root	the part of the plant that takes in water
stem	the part of the plant that moves water around the plant

Animals and Plants

by Shirley Horton

Animals Live in Different Habitats

Animals live in different places. Their body parts help them.

Polar bears can live in very cold places. They have fur. Fur helps keep them warm.

Some plants use camouflage like animals do. Some plants look like the ground. They are hard to find. They stay safe.

Now you know a lot about parts of animals and plants. What are some parts that keep them safe? What are some parts that help them get food?

Plants Stay Safe

Plants have many ways to stay safe. Some plants have spines or thorns. Spines and thorns can hurt animals. Animals do not want to eat these plants. Other plants have a bad taste or smell. That keeps animals away too.

Cactus

These animals help each other. Shrimp do not see very well. They can feel with their **antennae.** The shrimp feel the tails of the fish. The fish lead the shrimp.

Goby fish

Snapping shrimp

Animals Get Food

Animals use their body parts to get food. Some birds use beaks to eat. Some bird beaks can tear meat. Some bird beaks can open seeds and nuts. Animal teeth can break nuts too.

Hawk

Plants need water to grow. This plant lives in a desert. The desert does not have much water. The little leaves help keep water inside the plant.

Ocotillo

Plants in Different Habitats

Plants live in different places. Plants need light from the Sun to grow. This plant lives in a dark rain forest. The big leaves can take in lots of light for the plant.

Bears catch fish to eat. They use their claws and teeth. Zebras eat grass. Their flat teeth help them bite and chew.

Animals Stay Safe

Animals have different ways to stay safe. The colors and shapes of animals can protect them. **Camouflage** is a color or shape. It makes animals hard to see.

This toad uses camouflage.

Plant Parts

Plants are living things too. They have parts that help them live.

The roots take in water for the plant.

Praying mantis

This insect is hard to see. It looks like a plant stem with a leaf. Camouflage helps it hide from other animals. Camouflage also helps it get food.

Hiding in the Water

This big snake hides under water. Its nose and eyes are on top of the water. It waits for animals that come near the water. Then it pulls them in. The animals are its food.

Animals Warn of Danger

A rabbit can tell other rabbits that there is danger. It hits its back foot on the ground.

A prairie dog can tell other prairie dogs that there is danger too. It makes a loud bark.

Prairie dogs

Genre	Comprehension Skill	Text Features	Science Content
Nonfiction	Put Things in Order	• Captions • Diagrams • Labels • Glossary	Life Cycles

Scott Foresman Science 1.4

ISBN 0-328-13743-X
9 780328 137435 90000
scottforesman.com

Science

Life Science

Living Things Grow and Change

by Ann Rossi

What did you learn?

1. Name one way a tadpole is different from a grown frog.

2. What is the first step in the life cycle of a butterfly?

3. **Writing** in Science Most plants grow from seeds. Write to explain what happens as plants grow. Use words from the book as you write.

4. **Put Things in Order** A frog starts life as an egg. What happens next?

Vocabulary

larva
life cycle
pupa
seed coat
seedling
tadpole

Picture Credits
Every effort has been made to secure permission and provide appropriate credit for photographic material. The publisher deeply regrets any omission and pledges to correct errors called to its attention in subsequent editions.

Photo locators denoted as follows: Top (T), Center (C), Bottom (B), Left (L), Right (R), Background (Bkgd)

12 (BL) ©Tom Bean/Corbis

Scott Foresman/Dorling Kindersley would also like to thank: 3 (Bkgd) Stephen Oliver/DK Images.

Unless otherwise acknowledged, all photographs are the copyright © of Dorling Kindersley, a division of Pearson.

ISBN: 0-328-13743-X

2 3 4 5 6 7 8 9 10 V004 13 12 11 10 09 08 07 06 05

Glossary

larva a young insect

life cycle the ways living things change

pupa the stage between larva and butterfly in the life cycle of a butterfly

seed coat the outer covering of a seed

seedling a young plant

tadpole a young frog

Living Things Grow and Change

by Ann Rossi

Growing and Changing

Living things change as they grow. Animals change as they grow. Plants also change as they grow. These changes are the **life cycles** of living things.

Plants and animals are young when they start their life cycles. They change as they grow. Grown plants may make seeds. Grown animals may make eggs. Then life cycles begin again.

Plants Grow and Change

Sometimes flowers are the same colors, shapes, or sizes. Sometimes flowers are different from each other.

These flowers are lilies. Can you count the many ways these lilies are different?

The changes in a life cycle happen in order. A plant or animal begins life. Then it grows. It changes as it grows.

Frogs Grow

A frog begins as a tiny egg. The egg is in water. Soon the egg hatches. A **tadpole** swims out. A tadpole is a very young frog.

A tadpole does not look like a frog. A tadpole has a tail. Tadpoles swim in water.

Some trees grow cones. A pine tree grows cones. Seeds grow inside cones. Other trees grow flowers and fruit. Seeds grow inside fruit.

Trees Grow

Trees are plants. Trees grow and change. Most trees grow from seeds. First, the seed coat opens. Next, a seedling grows. The seedling grows into a tree after many years.

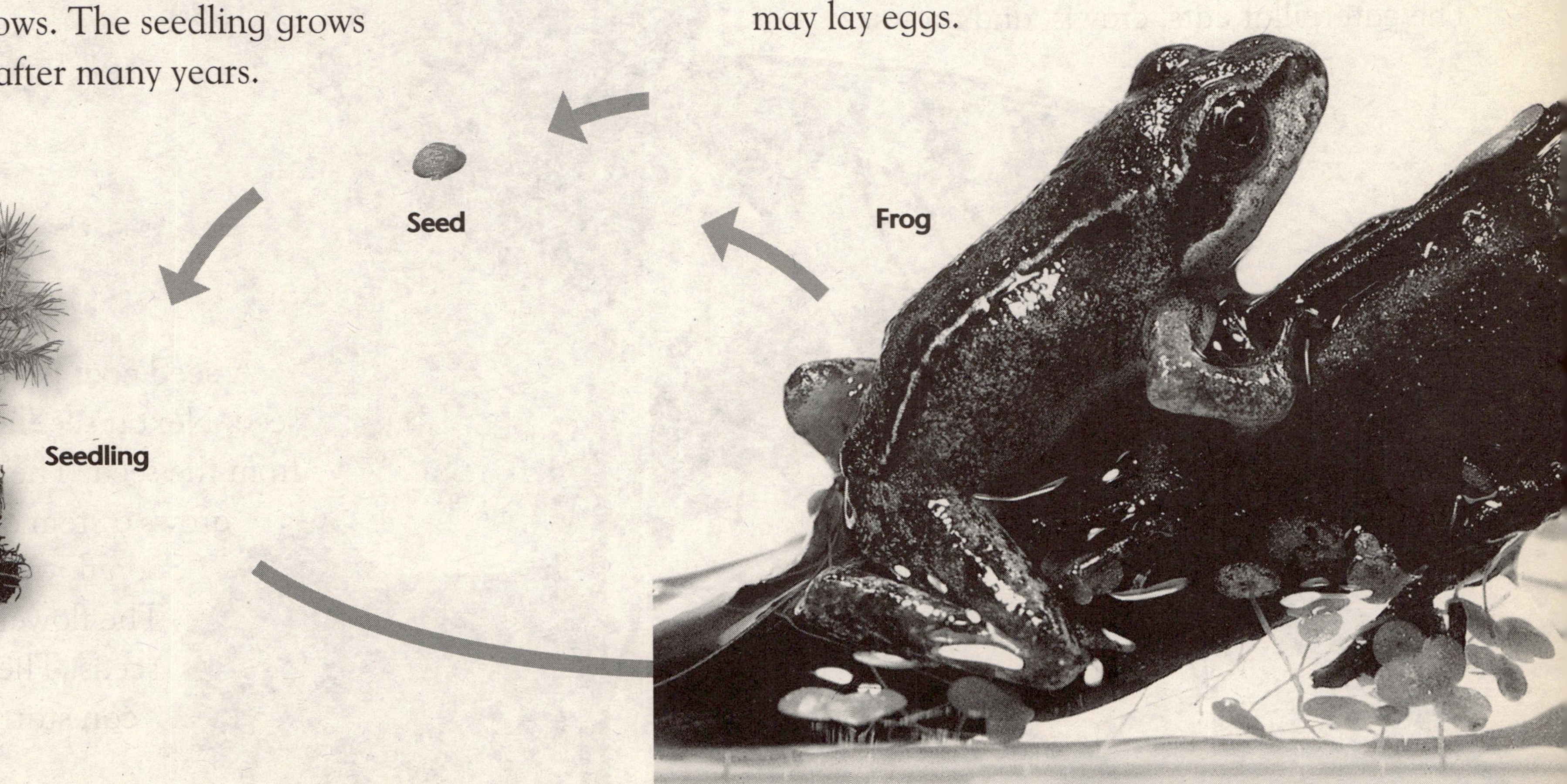

The tadpole eats, swims, and grows. Soon it grows back legs. Next it grows front legs. Then its tail is gone.

Soon the tadpole becomes a grown frog. The frog hops on land. It also swims in water. One day it may lay eggs.

Butterflies Grow

The butterfly also starts as a tiny egg. A young insect is called a **larva.** It hatches from the egg.

A butterfly larva is called a caterpillar. The caterpillar eats, crawls, and grows.

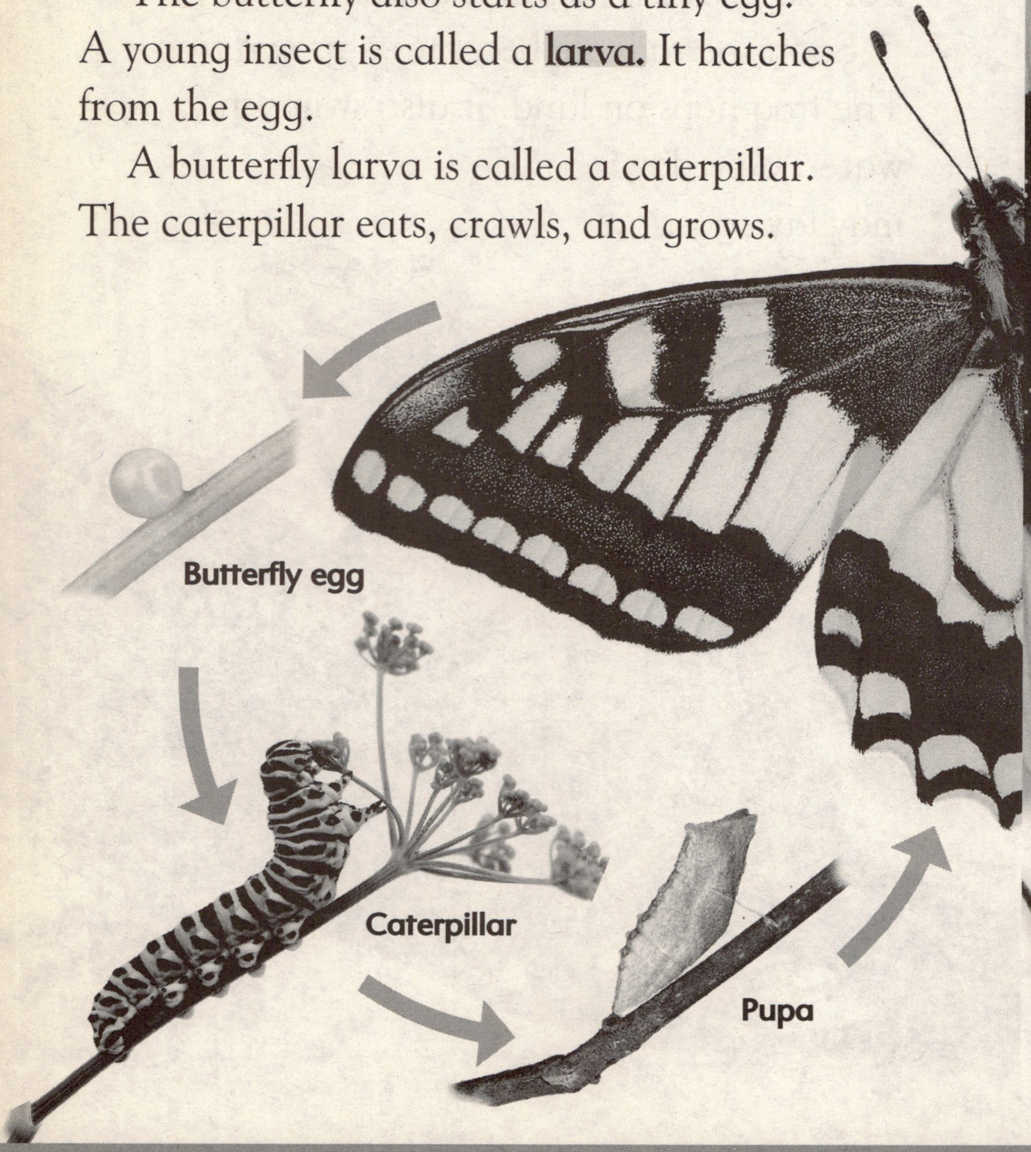

Butterfly egg

Caterpillar

Pupa

New sunflower seeds

A **seed coat** protects the seed. Next a **seedling** grows from the seed. The seedling grows a stem and roots. Soon flowers bloom. The flowers make seeds. The life cycle can start again.

Sunflowers Grow

A sunflower is a plant. Most plants grow from seeds. A sunflower does too. The life cycle of a sunflower starts with a seed.

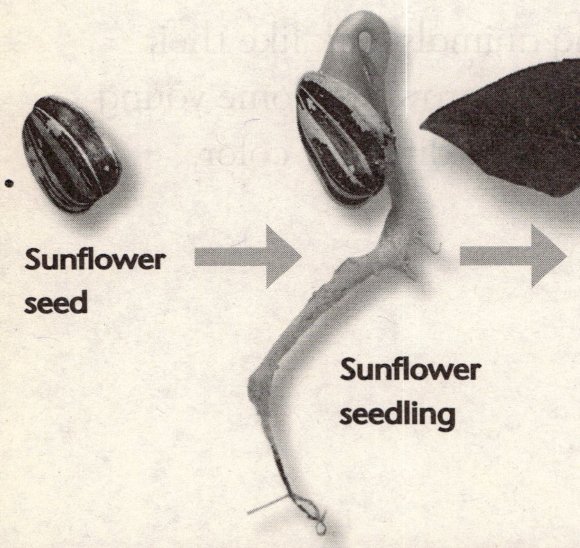

Sunflower seed

Sunflower seedling

Sunflower plant

Butterfly

The butterfly waits for its wings to dry.

The caterpillar changes to a **pupa.** It is inside a hard covering. The pupa changes into a butterfly. It comes out of the cover.

The butterfly has wings. It flies. The butterfly may lay eggs one day.

Animals Grow and Change

Young animals change as they grow. Their size may change. Their shape can change too.

A young newt has gills. Adult newts do not. Young and adult newts can be different colors.

Young newt

Adult newt

Some young animals look like their parents when they grow up. Some young animals may have a different color, pattern, or size.

Science

Genre	Comprehension Skill	Text Features	Science Content
Nonfiction	Draw Conclusions	• Call Outs • Captions • Labels • Glossary	Food Chains

Scott Foresman Science 1.5

ISBN 0-328-13746-4
9 780328 137466 90000

scottforesman.com

Science

Life Science

Food Chains and Habitats

by Ann Rossi

Vocabulary

food chain
marsh
oxygen
rain forest

Picture Credits
Every effort has been made to secure permission and provide appropriate credit for photographic material. The publisher deeply regrets any omission and pledges to correct errors called to its attention in subsequent editions.

Photo locators denoted as follows: Top (T), Center (C), Bottom (B), Left (L), Right (R), Background (Bkgd)

Opener: Tom Brakefield/Corbis; 1 Digital Vision; 8 (C) ©Philip Dowell/DK Images; 12 (TL) ©O.S.F./Animals Animals/Earth Scenes; 13 Tom Brakefield/Corbis; 14 (C) ©Philip Dowell/DK Images

Scott Foresman/Dorling Kindersley would also like to thank: 6 Stephen Oliver/©DK Images.

ISBN: 0-328-13746-4

2 3 4 5 6 7 8 9 10 V004 13 12 11 10 09 08 07 06 05

What did you learn?

1. What three things do green leaves need to make food?

2. What does a penguin eat in the Antarctic?

3. **Writing** in Science Some animals eat other animals. On your own paper, write to tell which animals in this book eat other animals. Use words from the book as you write.

4. **Draw Conclusions** Living things are connected in food chains. What happens if one part of a food chain changes?

Glossary

food chain the connection between living things and their food

marsh a wetland habitat

oxygen a gas in the air that plants and animals need to live

rain forest a habitat with tall trees and a lot of rain

Food Chains and Habitats

by Ann Rossi

Food For Living Things

All living things need food. You need food. Animals need food. Plants need food too!

Frog

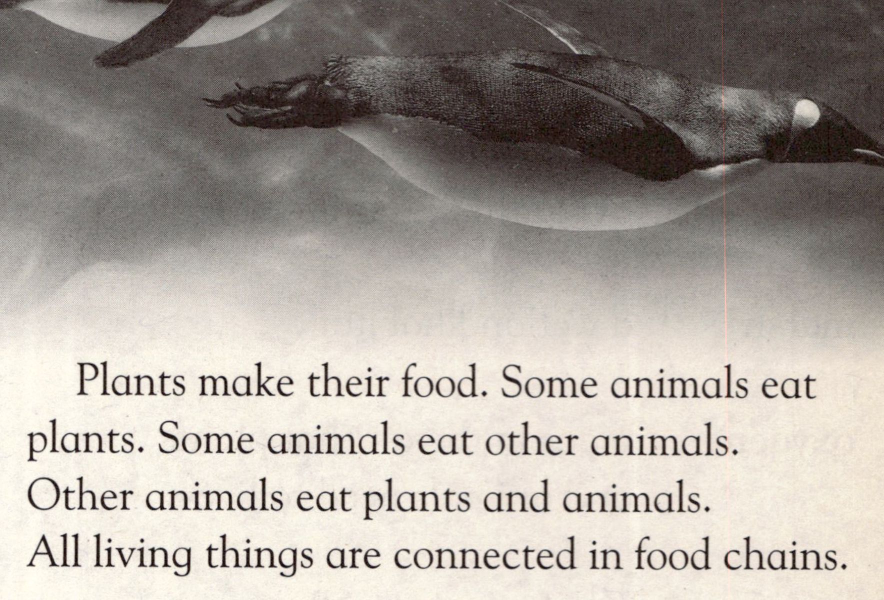

Plants make their food. Some animals eat plants. Some animals eat other animals. Other animals eat plants and animals. All living things are connected in food chains.

Living Things And Food Chains

Living things live in many habitats. Living things need to find food in their habitats.

Gray squirrels

How Animals Get Food

Some animals eat plants. Rabbits eat plants. Some animals eat other animals. Lions eat other animals. Some animals eat plants and animals. Skunks eat fruit, seeds, insects, and mice.

How Plants Get Food

Plants use their parts to make food. The leaves of green plants make food. They use light from the Sun, air, and water.

Penguins eat krill. Penguins swim to get them. Orca whales eat penguins they find in the water. This is an Antarctic food chain.

Plankton are living things. Some plankton use sunlight to make food. Krill are tiny animals like shrimp. They eat plankton.

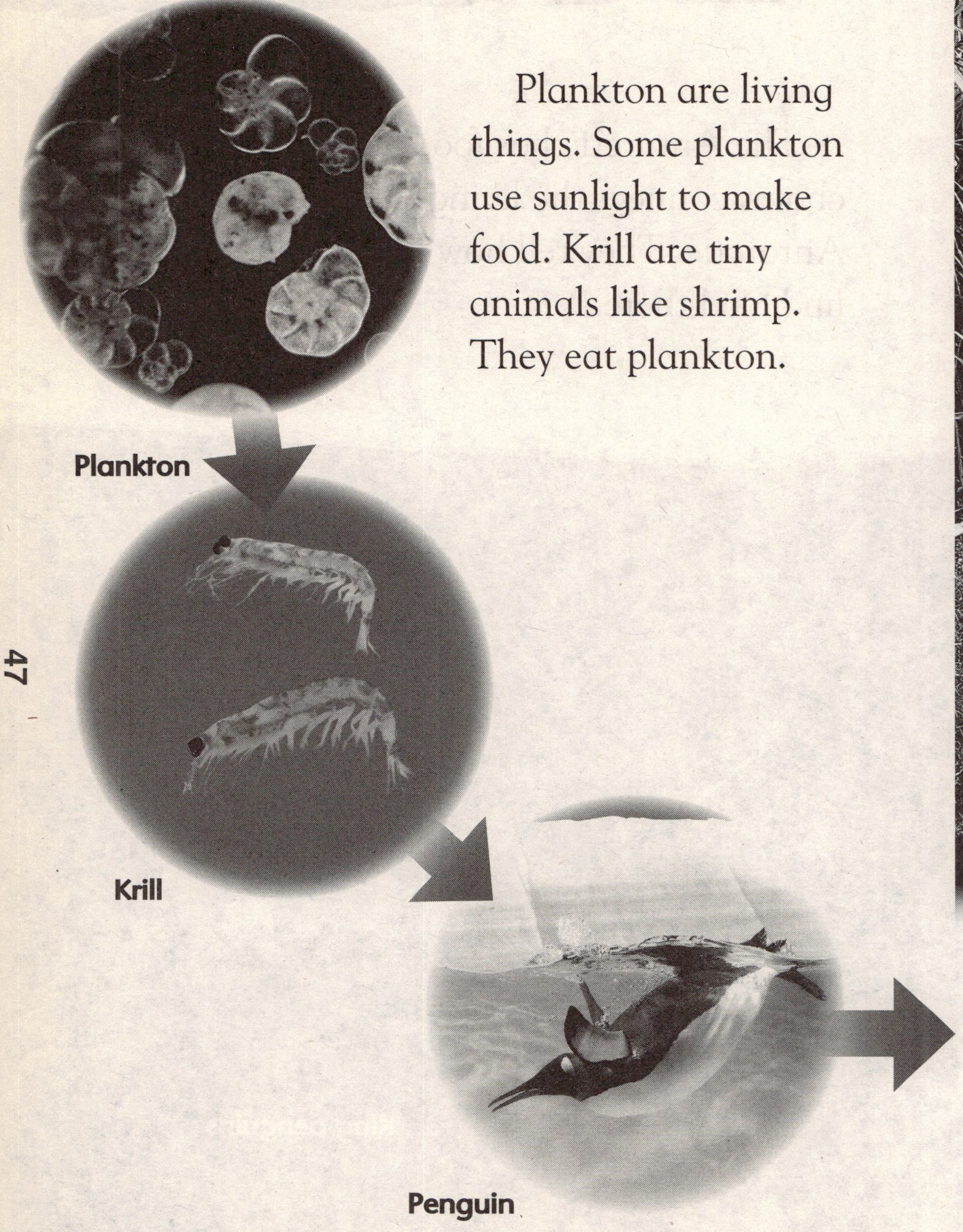

Plankton

Krill

Penguin

Sugar cane

Plant roots take in water. The stem takes water to the leaves. The green leaves take in sunlight and air. Now the green leaves have what they need to make food.

Food Chains

Plants make food, and food chains start. Plants give off oxygen when they make food. **Oxygen** is a gas in the air. Animals and plants need oxygen to live.

The Antarctic has food chains. Food chains connect the living things of the Antarctic. They tell how living things find food there.

King penguins

48

An Antarctic Food Chain

The Antarctic is a habitat. It is very cold. There are not as many living things there. But some plants and animals live in this habitat. Many live in the water.

Animals find food in their habitats. They need to eat other living things. Some animals eat plants. Other animals eat those animals. The link between living things and the food they eat is a **food chain.**

Some jaguars live in rain forests.

Food chains are in all habitats. A **rain forest** is a habitat. The Sun helps rain forest plants make food. Animals eat those plants. Other animals eat those animals. This makes a rain forest food chain.

A **marsh** is a wetland habitat. The Sun helps marsh plants make food too. Animals eat those plants. Other animals eat those animals. This makes a marsh food chain.

Some caimans live in marshes.

Science

Genre	Comprehension Skill	Text Features	Science Content
Nonfiction	Important Details	• Call Outs • Labels • Glossary	Natural Resources

Scott Foresman Science 1.6

ISBN 0-328-13749-9
9 780328 137497 90000

scottforesman.com

Science

Earth Science

Natural Resources

by Carol Levine

What did you learn?

1. What are three natural resources?

2. What are rocks of different sizes called?

3. **Writing** in Science Earth changes all the time. Write to describe the changes and how they can happen. Use words from the book as you write.

4. **Important Details** How do living things use land?

Vocabulary

clay
erosion
humus
minerals
natural resource
rocks
sand
weathering

Picture Credits
Every effort has been made to secure permission and provide appropriate credit for photographic material. The publisher deeply regrets any omission and pledges to correct errors called to its attention in subsequent editions.

Photo locators denoted as follows: Top (T), Center (C), Bottom (B), Left (L), Right (R), Background (Bkgd).

Opener: Getty Images; 1 (L, C) Getty Images, (R) Digital Vision; 4 Getty Images; 5 (T) Dr Jeremy Burgess/ Photo Researchers, Inc., (B) Getty Images; 9 Getty Images; 11 (T) Getty Images; 12 (TL, BR) Getty Images; 14 (L, C, R) Getty Images; 15 (C) © Paul Seheult/Eye Ubiquitous/Corbis, (TR) Getty Images.

Scott Foresman/Dorling Kindersley would also like to thank: 2 NASA/DK Images; 6 (BL) Stephen Oliver/DK Images.

ISBN: 0-328-13749-9

2 3 4 5 6 7 8 9 10 V004 13 12 11 10 09 08 07 06 05

Glossary

clay	a sticky kind or part of soil
erosion	when wind or water moves rocks and soil
humus	a part of soil that is made of things that were once alive
minerals	nonliving natural resources found in rocks and soil that people use
natural resource	a useful thing that comes from nature
rocks	nonliving natural resources that come from Earth
sand	very tiny pieces of broken rock
weathering	when water and ice change the size, shape, or color of rocks

by Carol Levine

Parts of Earth

Earth has many things we use. Useful things that come from nature are called **natural resources.** Some natural resources are air, water, and land. Natural resources are important to all living things.

Ways to Help

There are many ways to save natural resources. You can help!

Reduce means to use less. Reuse means to use again. Recycle means to make old things into new things. What can you do to help reduce, reuse, and recycle?

Saving Natural Resources

Air must be clean. Dirty air is bad for living things. We can help air stay clean. Water and land must be clean too. We all can help. Pick up litter and trash. Use less water when you can.

The surface of Earth is made up of land and water. Earth has more water than land. Land with water all around it is an island.

Kinds of Land

There are many kinds of land. Some land is flat. Plains are flat lands. Some land goes up. Hills and mountains go up.

Minerals

Minerals are nonliving things. They are natural resources in rocks and soil. Graphite is a mineral people use. It can be used to make the inside part of pencils.

Water

Living things use water. Water helps living things. How do you use water?

57

Land

Land is important too. Food for people can grow in soil. Some plants grow in soil. Many living things live on land.

Kinds of Water

There are many kinds of water. Ocean water covers a lot of Earth. Stream water runs on top of land.

Ocean

Stream

Rocks

Rocks are nonliving things. They come from Earth. Rocks are natural resources. Rocks can be different shapes. Rocks can be different sizes. Big rocks are boulders. Small rocks are pebbles. **Sand** is tiny pieces of broken rock.

Using Natural Resources

Living things use natural resources in different ways.

Air

We do not see air. We can feel air when it blows as wind. People, animals, and plants all need air to live.

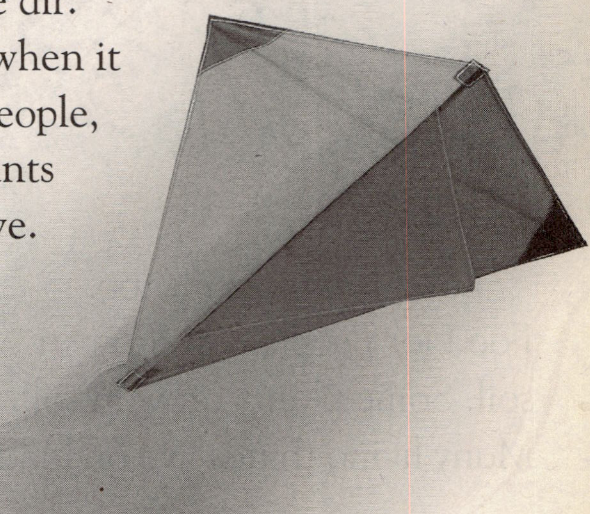

Sometimes erosion changes Earth. **Erosion** is when wind or water moves rocks and soil. A beach may look different after a big storm. There may be less sand. Erosion makes this change.

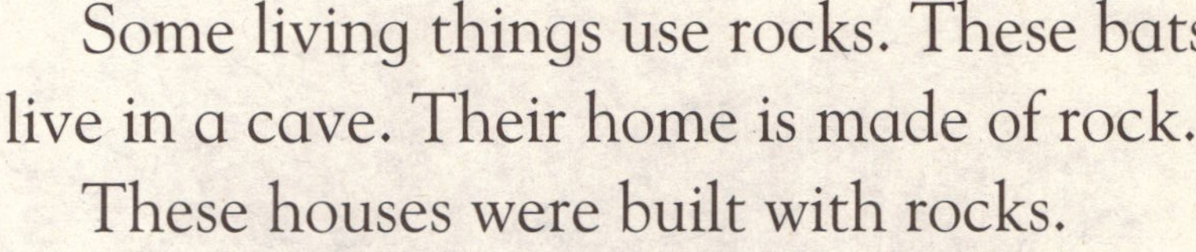

Some living things use rocks. These bats live in a cave. Their home is made of rock. These houses were built with rocks.

Soil

Part of Earth's land is soil. Soil is a natural resource.

Different kinds of soil look and feel different. Soil is made of different things. Sand and **clay** can be in soil. Humus can be in soil too. **Humus** is made of parts of things that were once living.

Land Changes

Land on Earth changes. Sometimes weathering changes land. **Weathering** is when water and ice break and change rocks. Weathering can change the shape, color, and size of rocks. These sea pebbles took a long time to get smooth.

Genre	Comprehension Skill	Text Features	Science Content
Nonfiction	Predict	• Captions • Diagram • Call Outs • Glossary	Weather

Scott Foresman Science 1.7

scottforesman.com

ISBN 0-328-13752-9

9 780328 137527 90000

Science

Earth Science

What Is Weather?

by Carol Levine

What did you learn?

1. What are some opposite kinds of weather?

2. What are some weather tools? What do they measure?

3. **Writing** in Science Clouds are made of tiny drops of water or pieces of ice. Write to explain how clouds are formed and what they can tell us about weather. Use words from the book as you write.

4. **Predict** You see a puddle on the ground on a sunny day. What do you think will happen to the puddle water later in the day?

Vocabulary

clouds
season
sleet
temperature
thermometer
water vapor
weather

Picture Credits
Every effort has been made to secure permission and provide appropriate credit for photographic material. The publisher deeply regrets any omission and pledges to correct errors called to its attention in subsequent editions.

Photo locators denoted as follows: Top (T), Center (C), Bottom (B), Left (L), Right (R), Background (Bkgd).

3 (L) Corbis; 6 Corbis; 9 Ted Russell/Alamy Images; 10 Brand X Pictures; 11 Digital Vision; 12 (CL) Brand X Pictures; 13 (CL, CR) Brand X Pictures; 14 (T, B, CL) Brand X Pictures.

ISBN: 0-328-13752-9

2 3 4 5 6 7 8 9 10 V004 13 12 11 10 09 08 07 06 05

Glossary

clouds	shapes in the sky made of tiny water drops or pieces of ice
season	one of the four times of the year
sleet	rain that freezes
temperature	how hot or cold something is
thermometer	a tool to measure the temperature
water vapor	water as a gas in the air
weather	what it is like outside

What Is Weather?

by Carol Levine

PEARSON Scott Foresman DK

Measuring Weather

What is it like outside where you live? What is the **weather** like today?

Weather is always changing. Living things find ways to live in all kinds of weather.

Look out the window. See what the weather is now. What do you think the weather will be tomorrow?

Seasons change in a pattern. Spring is before summer. Summer is before fall. Fall is before winter. Winter is before spring. Then the pattern starts again.

Weather changes all the time. Is it wet or dry? Are there clouds? Can you see the Sun? Is there wind? How hot or cold is it?

It is cold here.

It is hot here.

Temperature is how hot or cold something is. Temperature changes. We measure temperature using numbers.

The temperature is a higher number when it is hot. The temperature is a lower number when it is cold.

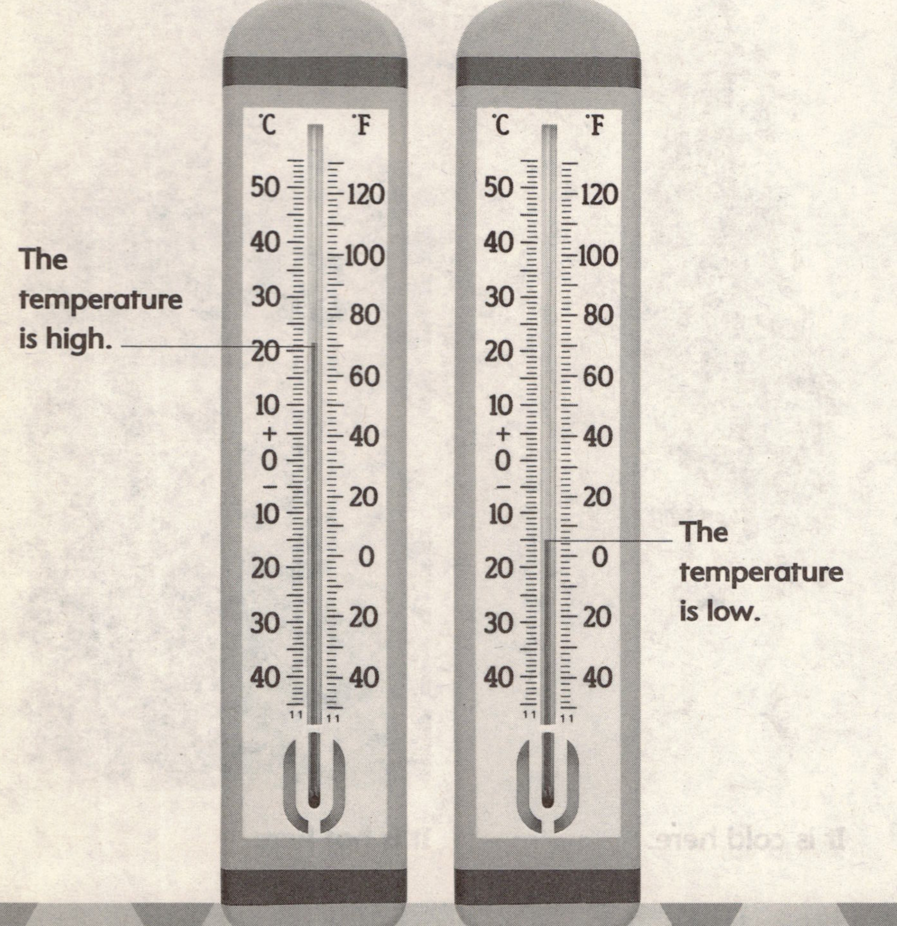

Seasons have different weather in different places. Spring can be warm. Summer can be hot. Fall can be cool. Winter can be cold. Winter can be very cold in some places.

Fall

Winter

Seasons

A **season** is a time of year. There are four seasons each year. They are spring, summer, fall, and winter. The seasons always come in the same order.

Spring

Summer

Weather Tools

There are many weather tools. A **thermometer** tells the temperature. It shows the numbers.

A wind vane tells which way the wind is blowing. A snow gauge tells how much snow falls. A rain gauge tells how much rain falls.

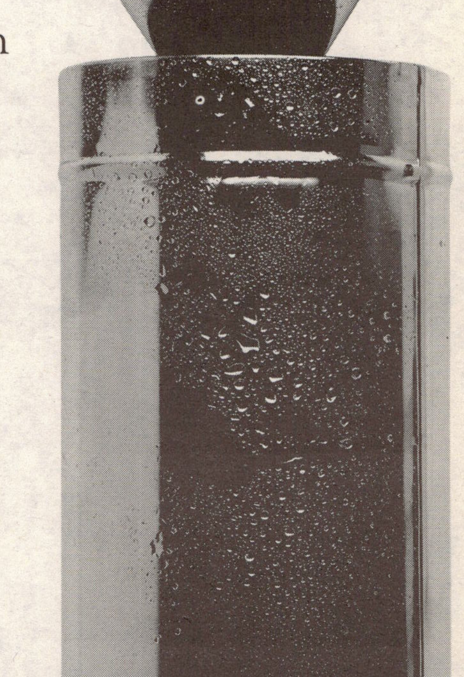

Wind vane

Rain gauge

Clouds

Water vapor is water in the air. You cannot see water vapor.

Clouds are made when water vapor cools. **Clouds** are made of many tiny drops of water or ice.

There are different kinds of snowstorms. There is lots of snow in a blizzard. Light snow that falls for a short time is called a flurry. A snow burst has lots of snow that falls quickly.

Snow

Snow is a kind of wet weather. Snow is water that freezes high in the air. It falls from the clouds when it is very cold. Many living things look for warm shelter when it snows.

There are many different kinds of clouds. Different clouds bring different weather. Most high clouds mean good weather. Most low clouds mean bad weather. Very low clouds make fog.

High clouds

Wet Weather

There are different kinds of wet weather. Wet weather can help living things. Plants need water from wet weather. But many living things look for shelter from wet weather.

Rain

Rain is a kind of wet weather. Some living things want to stay dry when it rains.

Sleet

Sleet is a kind of wet weather. Rain can turn to sleet when it is cold. **Sleet** is rain that freezes.

Science

Physical Science

Matter

by Arlene Block

Genre	Comprehension Skill	Text Features	Science Content
Nonfiction	Alike and Different	• Call Outs • Captions • Labels • Glossary	Matter

Scott Foresman Science 1.8

PEARSON
Scott Foresman
scottforesman.com

ISBN 0-328-13755-3
9 780328 137558 90000

Vocabulary

dissolve
evaporate
gas
liquid
mass
matter
solid

Picture Credits
Every effort has been made to secure permission and provide appropriate credit for photographic material. The publisher deeply regrets any omission and pledges to correct errors called to its attention in subsequent editions.

Unless otherwise acknowledged, all photographs are the copyright © of Dorling Kindersley, a division of Pearson.

ISBN: 0-328-13755-3

2 3 4 5 6 7 8 9 10 V004 13 12 11 10 09 08 07 06 05

What did you learn?

1. How can you describe solids?

2. Name a gas.

3. **Writing** in Science Matter can be changed. Write to explain some of the changes. Use words from the book as you write.

4. **Alike and Different** How are solids like liquids? How are they different?

Glossary

dissolve to spread through a liquid

evaporate to change from a liquid to a gas

gas matter that changes size and shape to fill the container it is in

liquid matter that changes shape to take the shape of its container

mass amount of matter in an object

matter anything that takes up space

solid matter that has its own shape

by Arlene Block

Matter

Look all around. Most of what you see is matter. **Matter** is anything that takes up space. Matter is made of tiny parts. Some parts are too small to see. **Mass** is the amount of matter in an object.

The book bag is matter.

Wood

Burning wood

Ash

Wood can burn. The wood becomes ash. It will not change back to wood.

What can you see that takes up space? This is matter. Matter is everywhere you look!

Other Ways Matter Changes

Some matter can change into a different kind of matter. The horseshoe is made of iron. The outside has changed to rust.

Iron horseshoe

Iron horseshoe with rust

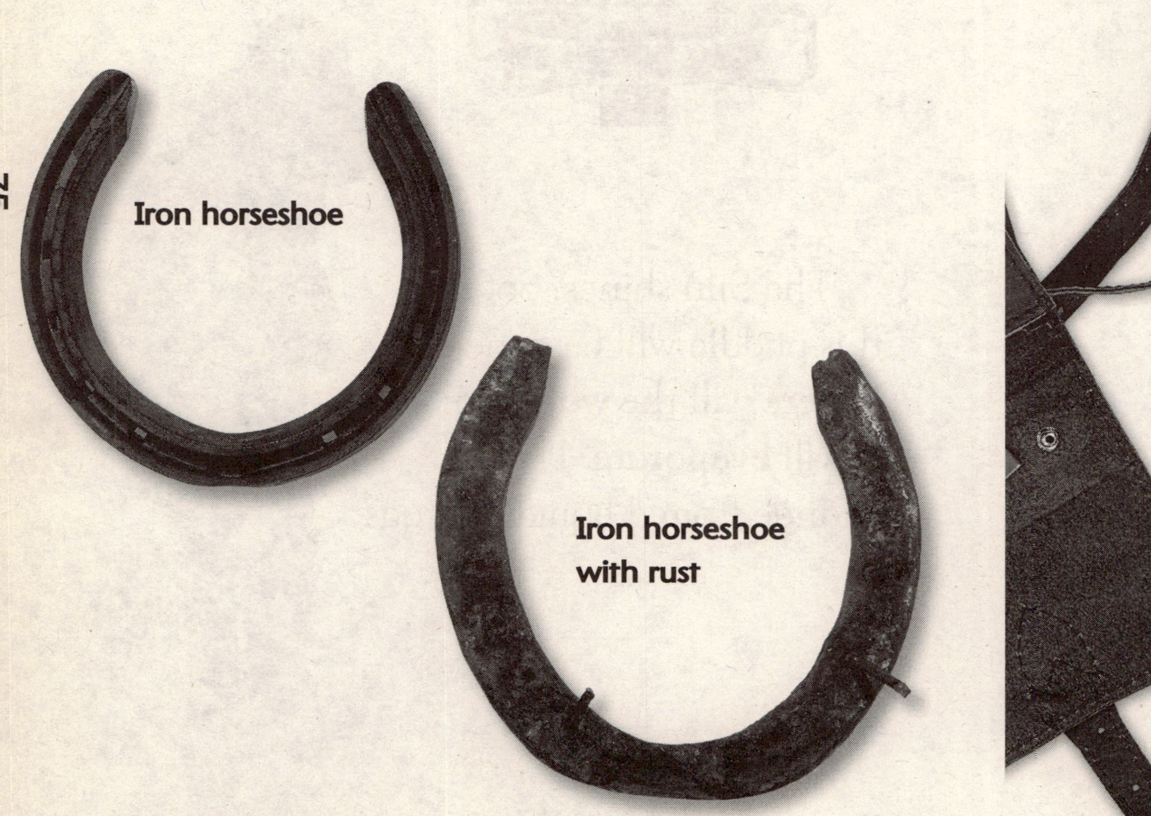

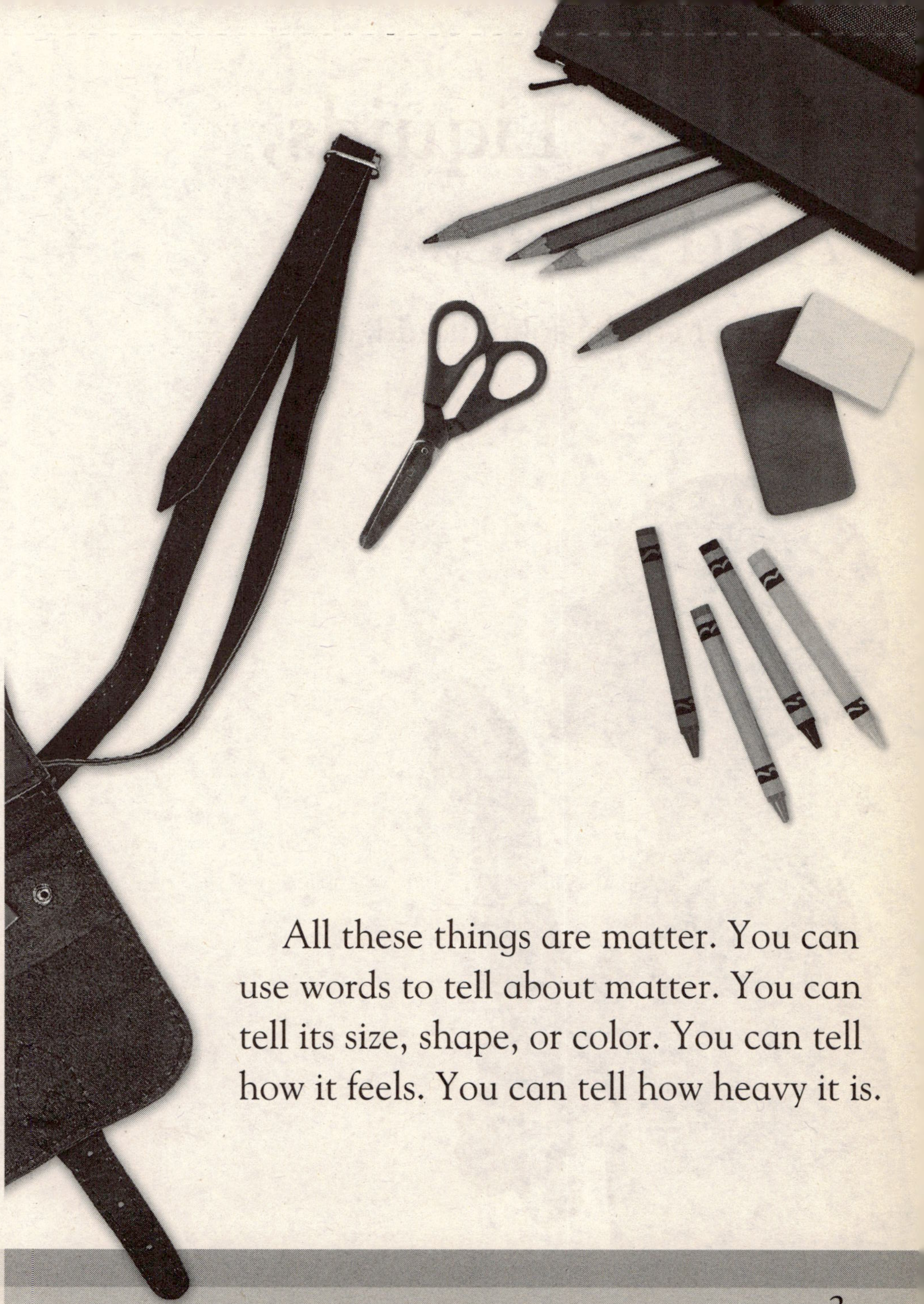

All these things are matter. You can use words to tell about matter. You can tell its size, shape, or color. You can tell how it feels. You can tell how heavy it is.

Solids, Liquids, And Gases

Matter can be **solid, liquid,** or **gas.**

Heat makes water boil. The water changes to water vapor. Water vapor is a gas.

The Sun shines. Soon this puddle will be gone. Where will the water go? It will **evaporate.** It will change from a liquid to a gas.

Water Changes

Water can be solid, liquid, or gas. Liquid water can freeze when it gets very cold. The water changes to ice.

Ice is a solid. Heat melts ice. The ice changes to water.

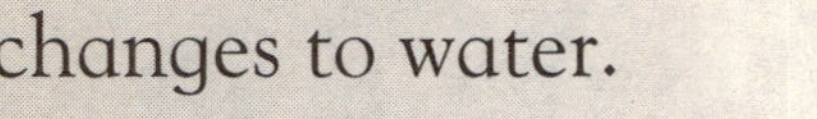

The basket is a solid.
These foods are solids too.

A solid takes up space. A solid has its own shape. You can move a solid. The shape will not change.

Juice is a liquid.

A liquid takes up space. It is different from a solid. A liquid can change shape. A liquid takes the shape of what holds it.

Powder paint

Water

Red paint

Some solids **dissolve** in liquids. The solid spreads through the liquid.

The water is a liquid. The powder is a solid. The solid dissolves in the liquid. It makes red paint.

What solids can you see?

You can mix matter. You can mix solids and liquids together. You can take the solids out.

A gas takes up space. A gas can change size and shape. Gas takes the size and shape of what holds it. You cannot see most gases. Air is a gas.

Gas is inside the balloons.

Matter Changes

Matter can be changed. The paper has one shape. You can cut it into new shapes.

This is a liquid. Pour it! Freeze it! A liquid can change to a solid.

A solid can melt. It can change to a liquid.

Science

Science

Physical Science

Forces and Sounds

by Carol Levine

Genre	Comprehension Skill	Text Feature	Science Content
Nonfiction	Cause and Effect	• Glossary	Forces and Sound

Scott Foresman Science 1.9

PEARSON
Scott Foresman
scottforesman.com

Vocabulary

attract
force
gravity
magnet
pole
repel
speed
vibrate

Picture Credits

Every effort has been made to secure permission and provide appropriate credit for photographic material. The publisher deeply regrets any omission and pledges to correct errors called to its attention in subsequent editions.

Photo locators denoted as follows: Top (T), Center (C), Bottom (B), Left (L), Right (R), Background (Bkgd).

3 (CR) Getty Images.

ISBN: 0-328-13758-8

2 3 4 5 6 7 8 9 10 V004 13 12 11 10 09 08 07 06 05

What did you learn?

1. What force makes a ball fall toward the ground?

2. How can force change the speed of something?

3. **Writing** in Science Magnets can repel and attract. Write to explain how magnets can do both. Use words from the book as you write.

4. **Cause and Effect** What would happen if you pressed a piano key very hard? What would happen if you pressed a piano key softly?

Glossary

attract to pull toward

force a push or a pull that makes something move

gravity a force that pulls things down toward the ground

magnet an object that can attract things made of some kinds of metal

poles ends of some magnets

repel to push away

speed how fast or slowly something moves

vibrate to move back and forth very fast

by Carol Levine

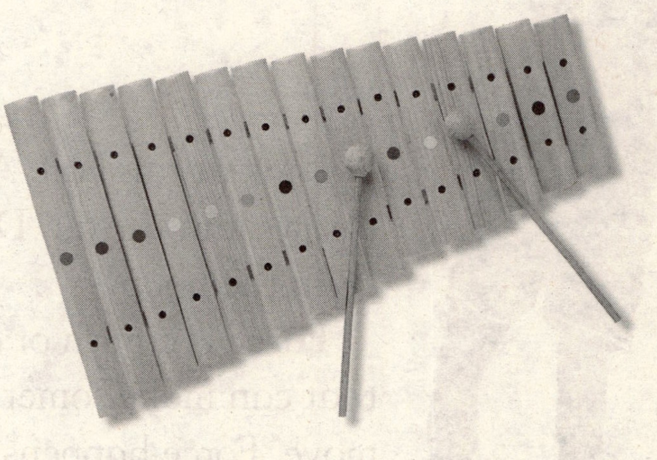

Moving

Look at this ball. A boy throws it in the air. Does it go in the hoop?

Force is a push or a pull that can make something move. Force happens when the boy throws the ball.

Things move. Sometimes this movement makes sound. Sometimes this movement puts things in different places. Movement and sound are all around!

Sounds are in nature. Suppose you are on this beach. You might hear birds chirping. You might hear the waves crashing. You might hear the wind blowing.

What happens when the ball drops? It falls. **Gravity** is a force that pulls things down toward the ground. Gravity pulls the ball down.

Using Force

Throw the ball hard. How far will it go? Throw the ball gently. Now how far will it go?

A hard push has more force. A gentle push has less force. Force can change the way things move.

Finding Sounds

Sounds are all around. Suppose you are in a toy store. You might hear a toy bell ringing. You might hear a toy drum playing. You might hear a toy car beeping. You might hear a grown-up saying it is time to go.

Making Sounds

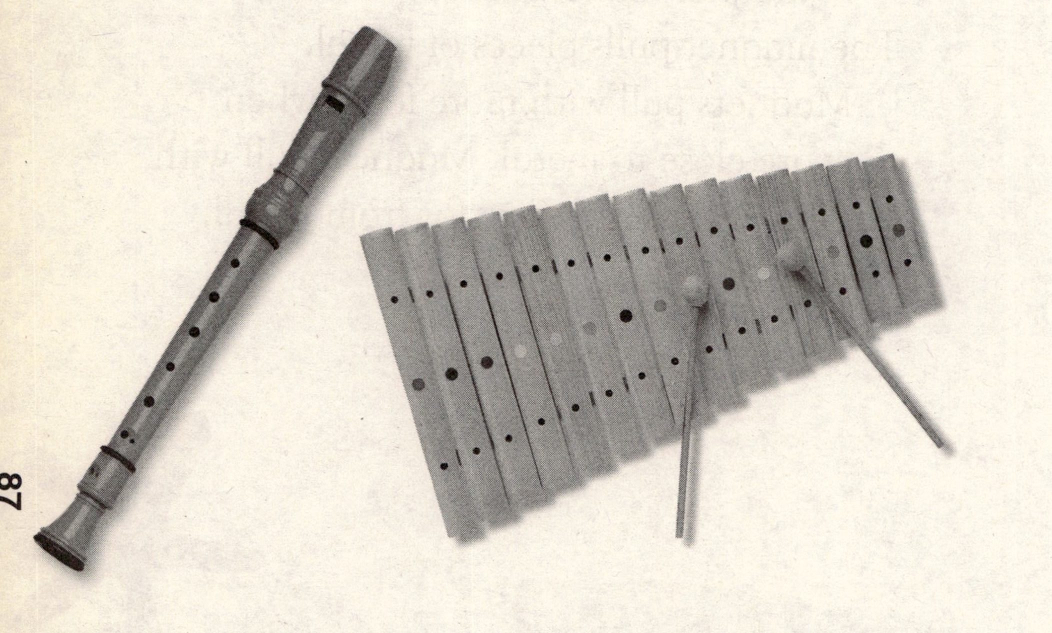

Look at these instruments. How do they make sounds?

When a sound is made something vibrates. **Vibrate** means to move back and forth very fast. Force changes sound. A strong tap makes a different sound than a light tap.

Speed

Speed is how fast or slowly something moves. Use more force. Things move faster. Use less force. Things move more slowly.

Ways to Move

Look at a skater move. She goes this way and that way on the ice.

She can jump up. She can bend down. She can go left. She can go right. She can go in a straight line.

A magnet makes this game work. The magnet pulls pieces of metal.

Magnets pull with more force when they are close to metal. Magnets pull with less force when they are far from metal.

Magnets

Look at the magnets staying up. A **magnet** attracts some kinds of metal. **Attract** means pull toward.

Magnets do not always attract. They can repel. **Repel** means to push away. Magnets may have two ends, or **poles.** Opposite poles attract. The same poles repel.

She can move in a curve.
She can even zigzag. She might fall.
Gravity pulls her to the ground.

Different Places

Look at these blocks. Can you tell where each block is?

The yellow block is above the red one. The blue block is below the green one. The yellow block is between the blue one and the red one.

The yellow block is next to the red one. The yellow block is on the floor. What will change if the blocks fall out of the bucket?

Science

Science

Genre	Comprehension Skill	Text Features	Science Content
Nonfiction	Draw Conclusions	• Captions • Labels • Glossary	Energy

Scott Foresman Science 1.10

scottforesman.com

ISBN 0-328-13761-8

9 780328 137619 90000

Physical Science

Energy

by Christine Wolf

Vocabulary

battery
electricity
energy
fuel
heat
shadow

Picture Credits
Every effort has been made to secure permission and provide appropriate credit for photographic material. The publisher deeply regrets any omission and pledges to correct errors called to its attention in subsequent editions.

Photo locators denoted as follows: Top (T), Center (C), Bottom (B), Left (L), Right (R), Background (Bkgd).

2 (B) Getty Images; 3 Getty Images; 4 (B) Getty Images; 6 (B) Getty Images; 8 (B) Getty Images; 9 Jim Pickerell/Alamy Images; 10 (B) Getty Images; 12 (B) Getty Images; 14 (TC) Peter Dazeley/Alamy Images, (C) Sally A. Morgan/Ecoscene/Corbis, (B) Getty Images; 15 (TC) ©Comstock Inc., (TR) Getty Images.

ISBN: 0-328-13761-8

2 3 4 5 6 7 8 9 10 V004 13 12 11 10 09 08 07 06 05

What did you learn?

1. What is the difference between a shadow when the Sun looks high in the sky and a shadow when the Sun looks low in the sky?

2. How can an electrical toy get the electricity it needs to work if it does not have a plug?

3. **Writing** in Science Energy in a house comes from many things. On your own paper, write to tell about energy found in a house. Use words from the book as you write.

4. **Draw Conclusions** You skipped breakfast this morning. You also forgot your lunchbox. After school, you feel tired and grumpy. What do you need to do to feel better? Why?

Glossary

battery something that stores energy

electricity something that makes street lights and other things work

energy something that can change things

fuel something burned to make heat or power

heat moves from warmer places and objects to cooler places and objects

shadow a dark shape made when something blocks the light

by Christine Wolf

Heat

Heat moves from warm places to cold places. Heat moves from warm things to cold things.

Look around you right now. You will see many things using energy. And you are using energy too!

Electricity

Battery

Food

Look at this house. Energy comes from all around. Can you name the things energy comes from?

Electricity

Gasoline

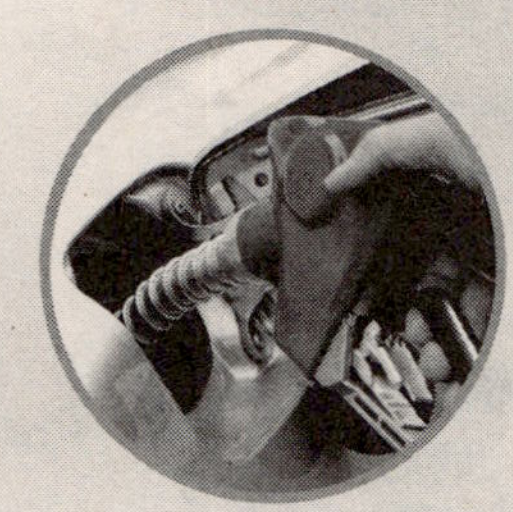

Wind

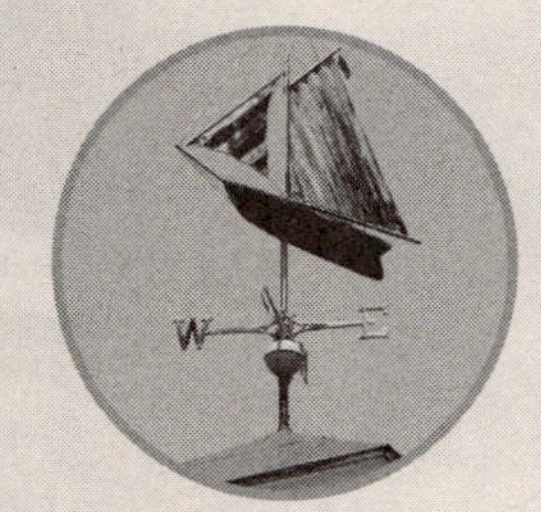

Heat can come from different things. Heat comes from the light of the Sun. Light from the Sun heats water and land.

Rub things together. This makes heat too. Moving also makes heat. Jump up and down. How does your body feel?

You use energy all the time! You use energy to play. You use energy to rest. You use energy to read this book. You even use energy to blink your eyes!

Energy for You

People need energy too. We need energy to grow, change, and move. People get energy from food.

Energy

The Sun gives light. Light is a kind of energy. **Energy** can change things. Energy from the Sun can change the temperature. More light makes things warmer.

Light and Shadows

Light comes from many things. Can you see light from the Sun? Is there a light in your room?

Electricity gives energy too. Energy from electricity makes things work.

Electricity moves from power lines to a plug. The energy moves into the cord from the plug.

A **battery** stores energy. This toy car uses energy from a battery.

Wind is moving air. Wind has energy. Energy from wind can make things move.

Making Shadows

Light can go through some things. Light cannot go through other things. A **shadow** is made when light is blocked.

Stand in the Sun's light. Your body blocks the light. The light cannot get to Earth. There is a shadow. It is the shape of you!

Changing Shadows

Shadows can change. Shadows are big if the light is close. Shadows are small if the light is far away. Shadows are different at different times of the day. Shadows are short when the Sun looks high in the sky. They are long when the Sun looks low in the sky.

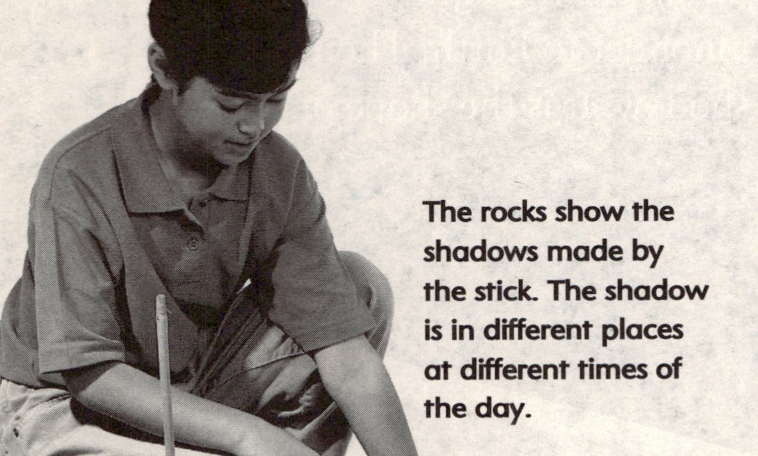

The rocks show the shadows made by the stick. The shadow is in different places at different times of the day.

Energy Around Us

There are different kinds of energy. A bus needs energy to move. It gets energy from fuel. **Fuel** is burned to make heat or power. Gasoline is fuel for the bus. Gasoline burns. Then the bus can move.

Genre	Comprehension Skill	Text Features	Science Content
Nonfiction	Important Details	• Call Outs • Captions • Diagrams • Glossary	Day and Night Sky

Scott Foresman Science 1.11

scottforesman.com

ISBN 0-328-13764-2
9 780328 137640 90000

Science

Science

Space and Technology

The Sky

by Lisa Oram

Vocabulary

Moon
planet
rotation
star
Sun
telescope

What did you learn?

1. What does Earth get from the Sun?

2. What do telescopes do?

3. **Writing** in Science Earth's rotation causes day and night. Write to explain why there is day and night. Use words from the book as you write.

4. **Important Details** How many planets that move around the Sun can you find in the picture on pages 12 and 13?

Picture Credits
Every effort has been made to secure permission and provide appropriate credit for photographic material. The publisher deeply regrets any omission and pledges to correct errors called to its attention in subsequent editions.

Photo locators denoted as follows: Top (T), Center (C), Bottom (B), Left (L), Right (R), Background (Bkgd).

Opener: (TC) Getty Images; 1 Getty Images; 2 (R) Getty Images; 3 (TL) Brand X Pictures, (TR) Getty Images; 5 (T) Diaphor Agency/Index Stock Imagery; 6 (B, Bkgd) Getty Images; 10 Getty Images; 14 (TL) Getty Images; 15 (BR) Getty Images.

Scott Foresman/Dorling Kindersley would also like to thank: 14 (CB, B), 15 (TL) NASA/DK Images.

ISBN: 0-328-13764-2

2 3 4 5 6 7 8 9 10 V004 13 12 11 10 09 08 07 06 05

Glossary

Moon a round object in the sky that moves around Earth

planet an object in the sky that moves around the Sun

rotation turning around and around

star a big ball of hot gas

Sun a big hot ball of gas that makes the day sky bright

telescope a tool to use to make things that are far away look closer

The Sky

by Lisa Oram

The Day Sky

Look up at the sky. What does it look like now?

The day sky and night sky are different. The sky is bright in the day. The **Sun** is a big ball of hot gas. It makes the day sky bright.

Humans have walked on the Moon.

The Sun lights part of the Moon. This is the part we see. The Moon looks different each night. It looks round and full. Then it looks thin. Then it looks full again. The Moon is full again every twenty-nine days or so.

Look up. What can you see in the sky now?

The Moon

The Moon is far away. But we do not need a telescope to see it. The Moon moves around Earth.

The Moon is not a planet. The Moon is not a star. The Moon has no air, plants, or animals.

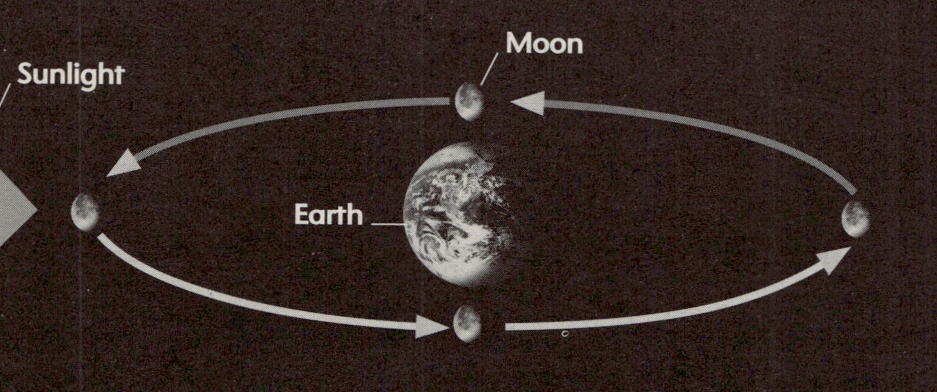

The Moon moves around Earth.

Sometimes you can see the Moon in the day sky. Most of the time you can see the Moon at night.

The Sun

The Sun is bigger than Earth. The Sun looks small to us. It is far away.

Earth gets light from the Sun. Earth gets heat from the Sun too.

Some planets are hard to see from Earth. **Telescopes** help people see things from far away. Telescopes make things in the sky look closer to Earth.

Earth is a **planet.** Earth moves around the Sun. Eight other planets do too. Planets do not give off light.

The Sun seems to move in the sky. This is because Earth is moving. Where is the Sun in the sky over you now?

Day and Night

Earth turns around and around. This is its **rotation.**

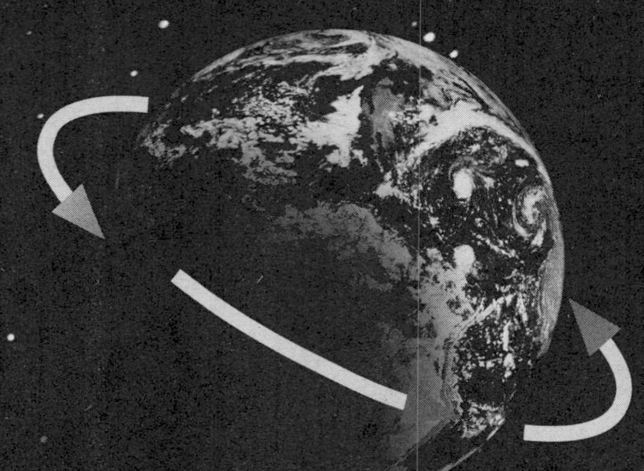

This cloud of gas is called a nebula.

A **star** is a ball of hot gas. Stars give off light. The Sun is a star. The Sun is the closest star to Earth.

Some people make wishes when they see stars!

The Night Sky

Sometimes, we can see stars in the night sky. We can see planets too.

One rotation takes Earth one day. We do not feel Earth moving. But it turns very fast!

Earth rotates. There is day and night. Part of Earth faces the Sun. Part of Earth faces away from the Sun. It is day for one part. It is night for the other part.

The flashlight is like the Sun. The globe is like Earth. The light shines on one side. When the globe turns, the other side gets the light. The side in the light has day.

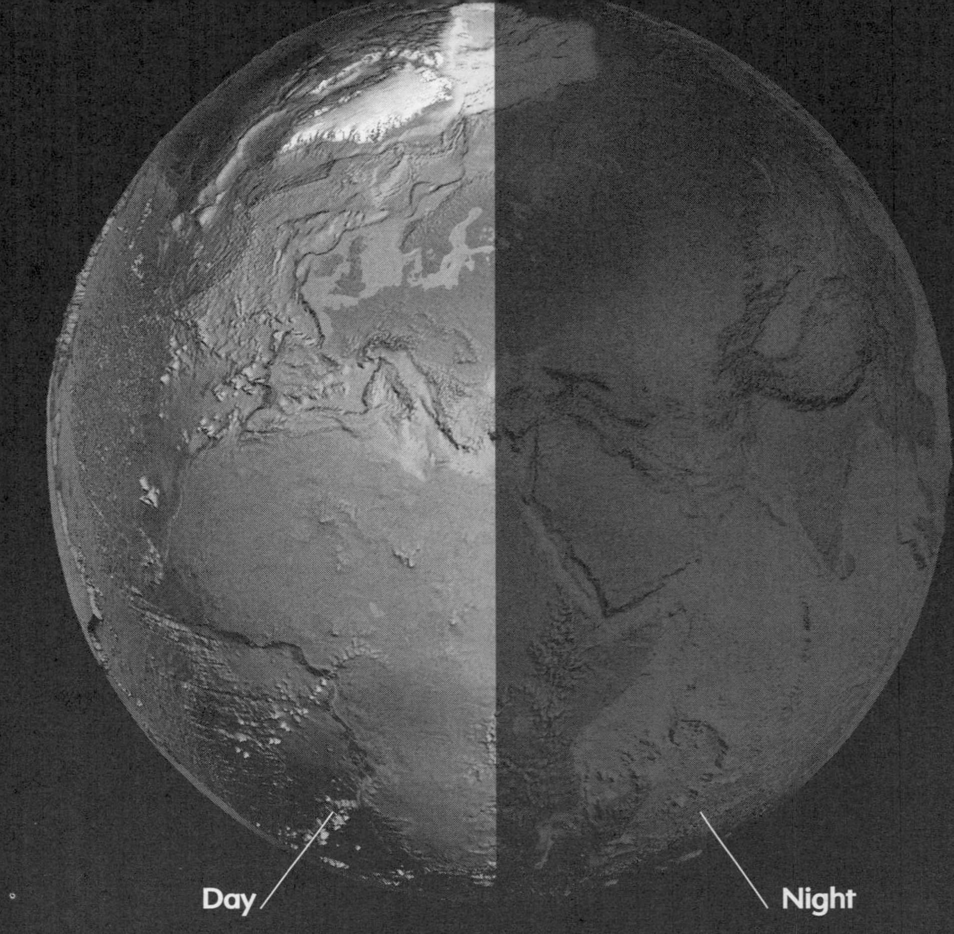

It is always day for half of Earth. It is always night for the other half of Earth. Day and night happen because Earth turns.

Genre	Comprehension Skill	Text Features	Science Content
Nonfiction	Put Things in Order	• Call Outs • Labels • Glossary	Technology

Scott Foresman Science 1.12

ISBN 0-328-13767-7
9 780328 137671 90000

scottforesman.com

Science

Science

Space and Technology

Science All Around

by Lily Samuels

Vocabulary

inclined plane
lever
pulley
screw
simple machine
technology
wedge
wheel and axle

What did you learn?

1. What do machines help farmers do?

2. What are some tools you can find in a kitchen?

3. **Writing** in Science Technology has changed over time. Write to name some of the machines and tools we use that people did not have long ago. Use words from the book as you write.

4. **Put Things in Order** Name the things that are done and the machines that are used as wood goes from the tree to the sawmill.

Picture Credits
Every effort has been made to secure permission and provide appropriate credit for photographic material. The publisher deeply regrets any omission and pledges to correct errors called to its attention in subsequent editions.

Photo locators denoted as follows: Top (T), Center (C), Bottom (B), Left (L), Right (R), Background (Bkgd).

1 Getty Images; 4 (CR) Age Fotostock; 5 Getty Images; 8 Lloyd Sutton/Masterfile Corporation; 9 George D. Lepp/Corbis; 15 Getty Images.

ISBN: 0-328-13767-7

2 3 4 5 6 7 8 9 10 V004 13 12 11 10 09 08 07 06 05

Glossary

inclined plane a simple machine with one high end and one low end

lever a simple machine that is used to lift something

pulley a simple machine that uses a wheel and rope to move things

screw a simple machine that holds things together

simple machine a tool with few or no moving parts that makes work easier

technology use of scientific knowledge to solve problems

wedge a simple machine used to push things apart

wheel and axle a simple machine used to move things

Science All Around

by Lily Samuels

PEARSON Scott Foresman DK

Growing Food

Food comes from many places. Some food grows on farms. Machines help farmers grow food. Machines are a kind of technology. **Technology** is using science to solve problems. Farming machines have changed over time.

Technology has changed. Long ago tools and machines were different. Look around your world. What tools and machines do you use?

Tools To Communicate

Long ago people did not have the technology we have now. There were no computers, cameras, televisions, or radios. Now we communicate using all these things.

Radio

Television

Computer

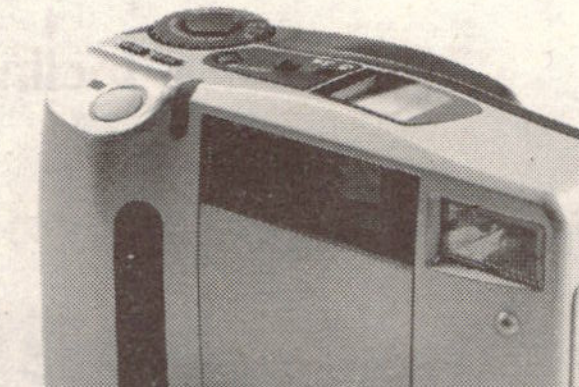

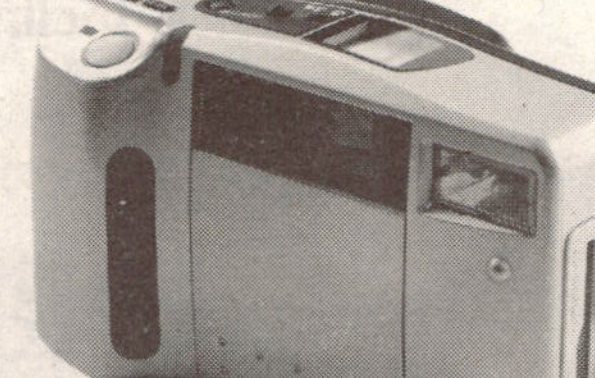

Camera

Seed drill

Planting and Growing Green Beans

Plows make the soil ready. Seed drills help farmers plant bean seeds. Machines make the work take less time. Machines make the work easier.

From the Farm To the Store

The beans grow. They are ready. The farmers will harvest the beans. Sometimes farmers use machines.

A pulley is a simple machine. A **pulley** can move things up and down. It uses a rope and wheel. Do you see two pulleys?

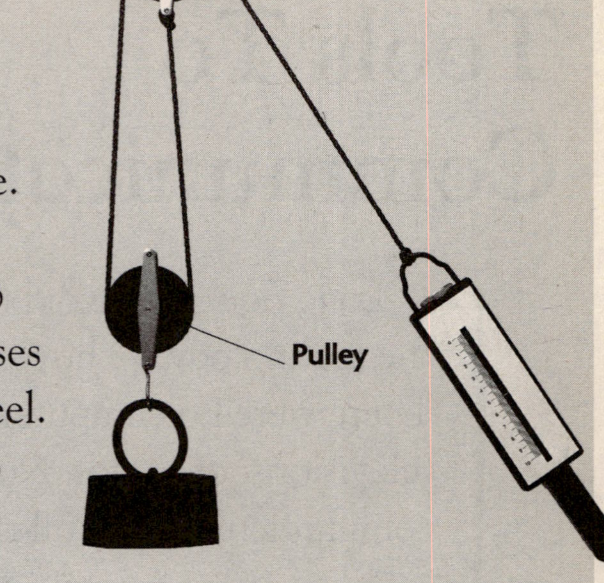

An inclined plane is a simple machine. An **inclined plane** is high at one end. It is low at the other end. It makes things easier to move.

Using Simple Machines

A screw is a simple machine. A **screw** is used to hold things together.

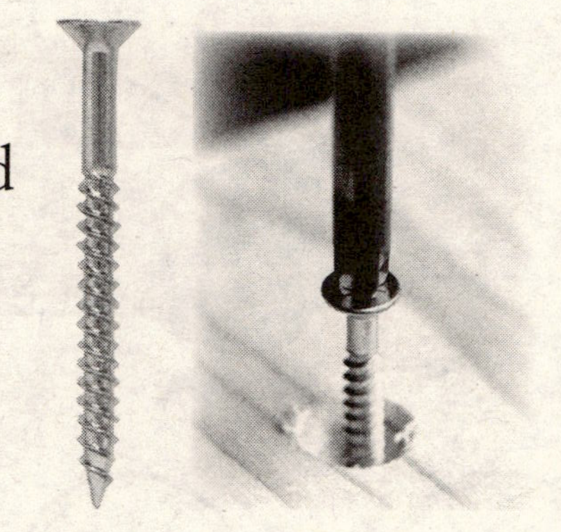

Screw

A lever is a simple machine. A **lever** is used to lift something.

The green beans are picked from the plant. They are put on a truck. Off they go to the store!

Tools to Make Dinner

Tools make work easier. Each tool does a different job. Let's make pizza for dinner! What tools do we need?

A wheel and axle is a simple machine. A **wheel and axle** is used to move things. The things on this page have wheels and axles.

Simple Machines

A **simple machine** is a tool. It has few or no moving parts. It makes work easier. Simple machines help do many different jobs.

A wedge is a simple machine. A **wedge** is used to push things apart. The red tool in the log is a wedge.

Serving Pizza

It is time to eat. Tools can help. What tools can we use to serve the pizza?

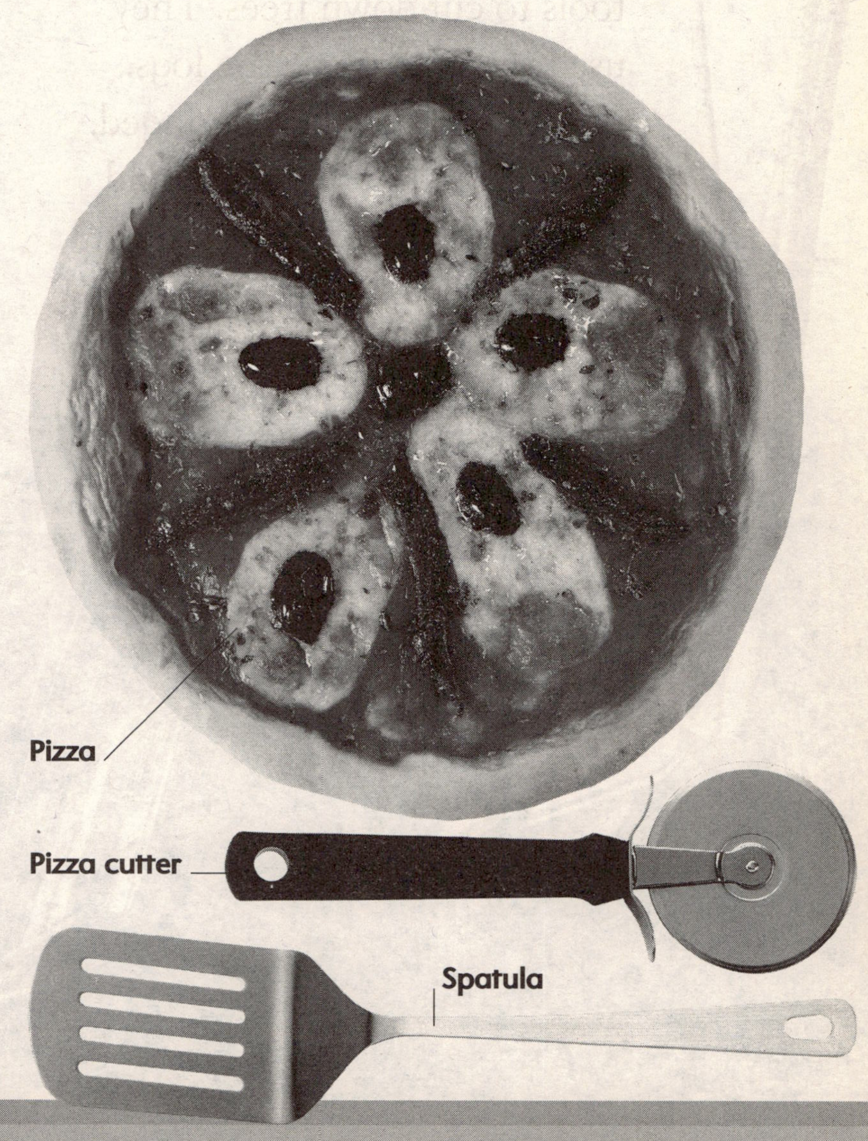

Getting Wood

Long ago people used hand tools to cut down trees. They used rivers to move the logs. Now technology has changed.

Big machines help cut and move logs. Tree shears help cut logs. Grapplers help move logs.

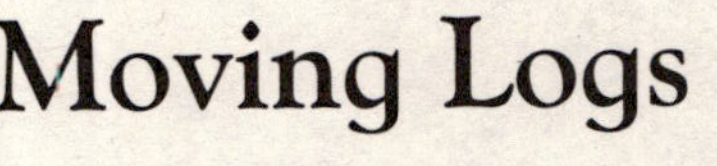

Moving Logs

Trucks take the logs to a sawmill. Machines help move the logs on and off the trucks. Machines also help cut the logs into boards.